START HERE

SIX FOUNDATIONAL LESSONS
FOR GROWTH IN CHRIST

♥

BY· LORI JOINER

Blessings!
Melanie!
Lori Joiner
Gal 2:20

cru✝

Cru Publishing
100 Lake Hart Drive 2500
Orlando, FL 32832

© 2014 Lori Joiner

All rights reserved. No part of this publication may be reproduced in any form without written permission from Lori Joiner, 1715 Grayson Lakes Blvd, Katy, TX 77494.

ISBN - 978-1-57334-094-6

Cover design by Traci Yau
Cover photo by Jelani Memory Photography - iStockphoto
Back cover head shot photo by Laura Chiles Atabala
Inside design by Andre Echevarria
Typeset in Adobe® Caslon Pro & Myriad Pro Light

This book is designed to provide accurate and authoritative information in regard to the subject matter covered. It is sold with the understanding that neither the author nor the publisher is engaged in rendering legal, counseling, or any other professional services. If legal advice or other professional advice, including counseling, is required, the services of a competent professional person should be sought. The author and publisher specifically disclaim any and all liability arising directly or indirectly from the use or application of any information contained in this book. Some of the anecdotal illustrations in this book are true to life and are included with the permission of the persons involved. All other illustrations are composites of real situations, and any resemblance of people living or dead is coincidental.

Unless otherwise identified, all Scripture quotations in this publication are taken from the Holy Bible, New International Version (NIV), Copyright 1973, 1978, 1984 by International Bible Society. Used by permission of Zondervan. All rights reserved.

Library of Congress Cataloging-in-Publication Data
Joiner, Lori, 1972-

Start Here / Lori Joiner

p. cm.

Includes bibliographical references

ISBN - 978-1-57334-094-6
Library of Congress Control Number:
1. Women—Growth 2. Religious aspects—Christianity
Printed in the United States of America

1 2 3 4 5 6 7 8 / 15 14 13 12 11

Contents

ACKNOWLEDGEMENTS

I am continually indebted to Jesus Christ for saving me, plucking me out of the miry clay, and setting my feet upon a firm foundation in Him. Without His constant guidance, love and direction I would be lost. Thank You, Lord Jesus, for rescuing me from a life that was headed down the wrong path and letting me have this one instead!

I am grateful for all the friends, past disciples, and fellow staff members with Campus Crusade for Christ® who gave me lots of great feedback and constructive criticism on the first few drafts of this book: Steve and Sarah Pogue, Casondra Brown Dewhart, Nikkea Jones, Ali Enos, Warren Culwell, and Lisa Mahan.

Thank you to my dear mom, Gerre Keller, for loving on my boys while I spent countless hours writing, re-writing, and working through edits.

Thank you to my loving husband, Alan, and sweet boys, Josh and Jake, for getting a little less of Mama while I finished this work.

Thank you to Sharon Morgan for letting me test out the first lesson on you!

Thank you to my dear partners in ministry with Cru who have supported me 19 years while I found my footing in women's ministry and labored along with me to students all over the world with the saving message of Jesus Christ.

 **PREFACE**

I distinctly remember sitting in a meeting at church when God spoke to my heart about this Bible study series. He even told me the name— *Start Here*. It was the answer to the question women repeatedly asked me: "What do I do with my disciple*?"

While I have been asked that question numerous times, not until that meeting was I in the place, mentally, to even think of writing another book. That very evening as I loaded my dishwasher, God poured ideas into my heart about what to include and how it should flow. I was *driven* to dry off my hands and begin typing. The kitchen was a wreck, but I was undaunted as I typed out the first lesson that night! I kept myself awake that night in bed, dreaming and praying and thinking of this book.

My favorite part about *Start Here* is that Jesus' words are the main text and starting point of each lesson—as if He is the One doing the discipling, He is the One teaching, and we are the learners. And He truly is, isn't he? He is our master discipler,* our teacher, our friend, our Savior, lover of our souls, the beginning and the end. I could not be more thankful and indebted for His guidance during this project.

I am so thankful you are holding this book. I am thrilled for what Jesus will teach you through these pages and what you will, in turn, teach to another woman. My vision is that this book will become your leader's guide for years to come, and you will disciple many women using this tool, helping to plant a firm foundation in the basics of the Christian faith.

So *Start Here,* sister!

*Denotes a word located in the glossary

START HERE

 **CHAPTER 1**

Jesus Demonstrates God's Love

Knowing how much God* loves us is foundational to a relationship with Him. He loves us. He has told us countless times in the Bible He loves us, He demonstrated His love toward us, and He taught us to love others. This lesson will explore God's love for us and identify key Bible passages where we learn of His love.

Passage Background

The Gospel* of John was written by John, one of Jesus'* closest followers. He was an eye witness to the teachings, miracles, and significant happenings in Jesus' life and recorded them in his book. Today we can read his words to gain special insight into the person of Jesus Christ. In the passage below, Jesus is talking to a religious leader named Nicodemus who sought Him out at night.

Nicodemus wanted to talk with Jesus personally and examine for himself the person and teachings of Christ. That conversation proved to be life-changing for Nicodemus. Later in Nicodemus' life he stood up for Jesus among his peers (John 7:50, 51). The key passage for this lesson is John 3:16, 17. This most likely is one of the most popular verses in all of Scripture. Seen so often on bumper stickers and signs at ball games, it easily can be overlooked as a profound declaration of God's love for us.

John 3:16, 17

¹⁶"For God so loved the world that He gave His one and only Son, that whoever believes in Him shall not perish but have eternal life. ¹⁷For God did not send His Son into the world to condemn the world, but to save the world through Him."

Digging Deeper

1. According to verse 16, what happens to people who believe in Jesus?

2. According to verse 17, why did God send Jesus to earth?

3. In verse 16, Jesus talks about eternal life. Find John 17:3 in your Bible. How does that verse define eternal life?

① No other Gods
② Don't say his name in vain
③ Keeping sabbath Holy
④ Honor Father & Mother   ⑤ Must not Murder   ⑧ Lie
⑥ " " commit adultry   ⑨ Covet House/wife
⑦ " " steal

Just to be Clear

1. According to verse 16, who loved first, us or God?

2. According to verse 17, did Jesus come to condemn the world?
   No, to Save the world.

It is significant to note that God loved people first. God loved us when we were not yet believers in Him, when we were sinful, when we were selfish, when we were prideful, etc. We did not need to do good things to receive God's love; He loved the world and sent Christ even before we were born. Furthermore, Jesus did not come to condemn the world, but to save it. He came to save us, not condemn us.

For Further Study

Read in your Bible John 15:9-13. Here is another passage from the Gospel of John that seems to bubble over with the love of God.

1. According to verse 9, how do we know Jesus loves us?
   He said 'So have I loved you'

2. According to verse 10, how do we remain in God's love?
   Keeping his commandments

3. According to verse 12, what is Jesus' commandment to us in this passage?   Love each other

4. According to verse 13, what is the greatest way to show your love for another?
   Selfless

Why do you think Jesus gave the command to love one another?

It makes everything else fall into place

What do you think is easy about that command?

It's easy to love good people

What do you think is difficult about that command?

Loving people who are difficult

How does it make you feel to know God wanted to make sure you knew He loved you?

A Few Pitfalls

From time to time some people encounter pitfalls when it comes to this topic. Two are addressed here.

1. A Wrong View of God

We have a choice when we read about God, His love for us, and what Jesus came to earth to do. We can believe what the Bible says: God is who He said He is and loves us as He said He does. Or we can continue to believe something else about God. Some women grew up in homes that were harsh, demanding, guilt-ridden, shameful or worse. Sadly, they project that onto God—they see Him as harsh, withholding, and demanding. Some women may see God as distant, aloof, silent, or not caring. God desires that his Son from heaven* to earth to reveal to us that He loves us, desires to be with us for eternity, and cares about us.

2. Lack of Reading Scripture* to Learn More About God

There is so much more about God than His love for us. In Scripture He reveals so much of His character, His forgiveness, His hatred of sin, and His miraculous interventions in the lives of people. Finding a time to regularly read the Bible is beneficial for women who have walked with God for some time and also for women new toa relationship with God. This dedicated, consistent time with God helps builds a view of Him based on Scripture. Just as someone gets to know another person by spending time with her, we need to spend time with God to grow in our understanding of Him and to have a correct view of Him.

This is our goal!

Can you think of other pitfalls women may face when trying to understand God's love?

If you were to describe God in your own words, what would you say? Would "loving" be an adjective you might use?

Present consistent

In Your Own Words

The new insights I learned about God's love are ...

*Reciprical Love
Rewarding*

The main message I gained from this lesson is ...

This new information will affect my life in this way ...

Action Steps for Next Week

o **Prayer:** Set aside time to talk with God through prayer each day. Consider praying a prayer of thankfulness to God for His love for you.

o **Bible:** Purchase a Bible (if you do not already own one). A Bible with study notes at the bottom or sides of the pages can help you understand the Scripture passages more easily. The *Life Application Bible* is a great option. Have a Christian friend explain to you how the Bible is organized and divided into two parts. Also have her show you how to look up books, chapters, and verses of Scripture.

o **Attend:** Meet with other women who believe in God. They can be a great encouragement as you grow in your relationship with Christ. Ask a trusted friend where she attends church or Bible study and consider attending with her this week.

o **Others:** Look for ways you can demonstrate His love by helping and caring for someone in need. This might mean babysitting, giving a ride, taking a meal, lending a hand, or calling a friend and offering her an encouraging word or just a listening ear.

o **Memorize:** Recite John 3:16 each day. By committing to memory key passages of Scripture you will always be able to recall that Scripture when needed for encouragement or for sharing with another to help her spiritually.

Prayer Journal

This space can be used to write a prayer to God, to record items you are praying about and the date they are answered, or to keep track of others you want to pray for.

_____

_____

_____

_____

_____

_____

_____

_____

Personally Speaking

I think John 3:16 was the first verse I memorized as a new Christian. I was 16 years old and had been invited to church by some friends. The youth director of that church shared God's love with me. Having a personal relationship with Christ and being convinced of God's love for me has had a tremendous impact on my life.

Knowing deep in my heart that God loves me has freed me up in life to take risks and walk in faith. If I did not believe He loved me or what He said in Scripture about His love for me, I could have frozen in fear at so many uncertainties in my walk with Him.

Another fantastic passage of Scripture about God's love is 1 John 4:7-21. Take a moment to find and read it now if you can.

My favorite verse from that passage is 1 John 4:10.

> "This is love: not that we loved God, but that He loved us and sent His Son as an atoning sacrifice for our sins."

The entire passage is such a clear, beautiful declaration of His love for us: that God is love, that God loved us first!

As I look back on my life, I know it was His love for me that helped me take that very shaky step to go "all in" to full-time ministry as a recent college graduate. To rely on Him to raise all of my financial support was a fearful, white-knuckled decision—one I could not have moved forward in without being totally convinced of His love for me. Embracing His love for me helped me through many years of painful singleness and sustains me even now as a wife and mother.

God is love, and He loves us. What a paramount truth to embrace as we grow in our relationship with Him. It is my hope that you and I grow in His love more and more every day, that His love overflows from our hearts onto others, and that it has a ripple effect to lives around us—one we may never see!

How about you? What would be different in your life and future if you were fully convinced of His relentless, unchanging love for you? What risks might you take if you completely embraced and believed He loves you?

 **CHAPTER 2**

Jesus Is the Way to the Father

Beginning a personal relationship with Jesus Christ is the most important decision you ever will make. Whether you are just starting your relationship with Christ, still having questions about trusting Christ, or simply wanting to know key passages in the Bible that point to security in your life in Christ, you are in the right place.

Passage Background

John, a follower and disciple* of Jesus, probably was His closest friend while Jesus lived on earth. John wrote his book to new Christians, repeatedly explaining throughout that Jesus is the special and unique Son of God, and all who believe in Him will have eternal life. At this point in the Gospel of John, Jesus knows His time on earth is drawing to a close, and soon He will be put to death on the cross. Jesus utters the following words during a special last time with his disciples. After eating a meal with them known as the Last Supper, Jesus dropped to His knees to wash His disciples' feet. Following that, He emphasized that He is the way to the Father.

John 14:1-6

[1]"Don't let your hearts be troubled. Trust in God, and trust also in Me. [2]There is more than enough room in my Father's home. If this were not so, would I have told you that I am going to prepare a place for you? [3]When everything is ready, I will come and get you, so that you will always be with Me where I am. [4]And you know the way to where I am going."

[5]"No, we don't know, Lord," Thomas said. "We have no idea where You are going, so how can we know the way?"

[6]Jesus told him, "I am the way, the truth, and the life. No one can come to the Father except through Me." (New Living Translation)

Digging Deeper

1. In verse 1, who does Jesus want us to trust?

2. In verse 6, how does Jesus say a person comes to the Father?

This verse uses phrases such as "Father's home," "more than enough room," and "preparing a place for you." When you think of heaven—the place where people who have a relationship with God will be for eternity—what words or pictures come to your mind?

Key Verse John 14:6

"Jesus told him ..." Jesus is talking to His most beloved friends, explaining He is the way to the Father.

"... I am the way ..." He is our path to the Father. He is not "a" way; He says He is *the* way, the only way.

"... the truth ..." He is the very essence of truth, and one need search no longer for the true way to God.

"... and the life." He is the way to eternal life; He has power over life and death. In Him we find purpose for our life and need not search any longer.

"No one can come to the Father except through Me." He was hours from giving His perfect, sinless life for us. His sacrifice on our behalf and our faith in Him is the only acceptable form of entrance into heaven.

In the Old Testament* God used animal sacrifice and the shedding of their blood as a payment for the sins of people. In the New Testament* Jesus became the perfect sacrifice once and for all.

Just to be Clear

In John 14:6, did Jesus open the door for other ways that could to lead to God?

Why Is He the Only Way?

> "For Christ also died for sins once for all, the just for the unjust, so that He might bring us to God, having been put to death in the flesh, but made alive in the spirit"(I Peter 3:18, New American Standard Bible).

He is the only way to God because He took the punishment we deserved by dying on our behalf. When Christ died on the cross (a typical method of capital punishment at that time), He did it for us, in our place. This is significant because He did not deserve to die. He had committed no sin or crime and yet willingly went to the cross to die for us, in our place, taking our punishment for sin upon Himself. When we place our trust in Christ, we acknowledge with our hearts that we know we are sinners, we need His forgiveness, and we are thankful for His death on our behalf. We can know Him personally now, and further, spend eternity being with Him and knowing Him even more!

For Further Study

Read Ephesians 2:8, 9 in your Bible.

1. **Grace** means unmerited favor or an undeserved gift. How is a relationship with Jesus an undeserved gift?

2. **Saved** is a term used to describe a person who has a personal relationship with Jesus. By placing our trust in Jesus Christ, we are saved from hell. According to this verse, how are we saved?

3. **Faith** means to believe in or trust in. Who are we to have faith in?

4. **Works** means good things done in hopes of earning God's favor. According to this verse, is salvation based on our good works?

What are some good works people may try to rely on to be saved?

What were you relying on before you heard about Jesus being the way?

How hard or easy is it for you to believe that good works or being a good person is not the way to eternal life with Jesus?

A Few Pitfalls

From time to time some people encounter pitfalls when it comes to this topic. Three are addressed here.

1. **Believing You Can Earn Your Way to Heaven by Being a Good Person**

   The way to Jesus is not about goodness or badness; it is about a decision to believe what He said about Himself: that He is the way to God, and He is God. The bottom line is that goodness, charity, volunteerism, church attendance, spiritual rituals, etc. will not save a person. It is confidence and trust in Jesus that saves a person.

2. **Thinking You Have to Trust Christ Again Each Time You Sin**

   Revelation 3:20 Jesus says, "Behold, I stand at the door and knock; if anyone hears My voice and opens the door,

I will come in to him and will dine with him, and he with Me" (NASB). Once a person places her trust in Jesus by inviting Him into her life, it no longer is necessary to repeat this process and reinvite Him in.

Simply put, there is no need to ask Him to come into your life if He already is there. Jesus said He never would leave us or forsake us (see Hebrews 13:5). Even when you sin, you can be confident the decision to place your faith and trust in Christ need happen only once. If you sin, you need to repent (turn away from your sin) and ask God to forgive you to restore your fellowship with God, but Christ has not left you.

3. Doubting Your Sincerity When You Placed Your Faith in Christ

This can be troubling for many people who sincerely put their faith in Christ. A person may look back with doubt, feeling deeply troubled, wondering, "Did I really mean it?" If this troubles you, consider two things. First, if you doubt your sincerity or doubt your salvation, then you can, once and for all (perhaps with another Christian), pray sincerely again. Second, if doubts surface again, consider them a ploy of Satan* to keep you from freely enjoying your relationship with Christ and the security you have in Him. You need to fight the temptation to dwell on the tempting thoughts of doubt and instead recite Scripture to counter the thoughts. Reflect on a verse such as John 1:12, "But to all who believed Him and accepted Him, He gave the right to become children of God." Then say to yourself, "I have believed on Him, I have accepted Him, I am a child of God, case closed!"

Which one of these pitfalls stands out to you the most?

Do you feel there are other pitfalls people may fall into?

How to Begin a Relationship With God

Placing your faith and trust in Christ is an attitude of your heart and an act of your will. You place your faith in Christ by making a decision to trust Him for forgiveness of your sins and for eternal life. This can be done by talking to God through prayer (out loud or silently). Here is a sample prayer:

> *Lord Jesus, I want to know You personally. Thank You for dying on the cross to pay the penalty of my sins. I give You my life and receive You as my Savior and Lord. Thank You for forgiving my sins and giving me eternal life. Make me the kind of person You want me to be.*

Have you trusted that Jesus is the way to God?

- o If not, would you like to do that today? If so, and the above prayer expresses the desire of your heart, simply pause here and pray this to Jesus right now.

- o If so, when did you trust Christ?

Why is it important for a person to know when she placed her faith in Christ?

In Your Own Words

The new insights I learned about faith in Jesus Christ are ...

The main message I gained from this lesson is ...

This new information will affect my life in this way ...

Action Steps for Next Week

○ **Prayer**: Consider praying a prayer of thankfulness to Christ for His death on your behalf.

○ **Bible**: Look up the Gospel of John in your Bible. Read the first four chapters this week. By the end of *Start Here* you will have read one entire book of the New Testament (just a few chapters week by week)! This book is a terrific place to start reading about the life of Christ.

○ **The Last Supper**: In the passage background of this chapter, the Last Supper is mentioned. Today it is known as the Lord's Supper or communion. In church services you will have the opportunity to participate in the Lord's Supper. This is a wonderful way for followers of Jesus to remember His death for us. The Lord's Supper consists of eating a small piece of bread that symbolizes His body being broken for us and drinking a small cup of grape juice (some churches use wine) as a symbol of Jesus' blood being poured out on our behalf. Perhaps your church will offer the Lord's Supper this week. If not, look for the next opportunity that presents itself for you to partake in this special commemoration of our Lord's sacrifice for us.

- o **Others**: People are searching for purpose and fulfillment in their lives. A relationship with Jesus Christ helps with both. Look for opportunities to simply share about your relationship with Christ and how He helped or encouraged you recently.

- o **Memorize**: Recite John 14:6 each day until you know it by heart. Also continue to review last week's verse. You may consider writing them on a note card and taping it to your mirror or dash in your car for easy reference.

Prayer Journal

This space can be used to write a prayer to God, to record items you are praying about and the date they are answered, or to keep track of others you want to pray for.

_____

_____

_____

_____

_____

_____

_____

_____

Personally Speaking

When I first trusted Jesus as my Lord and Savior at the age of 16, the idea of Jesus being the only way to the Father was not even a thought in my head. I simply and deeply wanted His forgiveness for my sins and to spend eternity with Him when I died one day.

As the years unfolded, and I grew in my faith and began regularly reading the Bible, I learned that He was, in fact, the only way to the Father. Further, I learned that I could not "earn" my way to heaven. This knowledge proved helpful as I began to travel in my mission work and talk about Jesus Christ to people in other countries and from different backgrounds. The idea that people can go to heaven if they are a "good person" permeates every people group I have had the privilege of meeting.

There is a problem with this way of thinking: How would we ever know if we were good enough? For example, if I told 50 lies in my life, but you told 100, then I guess I was better than you, and I would attain heaven. On the other hand, if you had 60 jealous or lustful thoughts, but I had 150, then you would be in heaven and not me. See the problem? Goodness is so subjective. Everyone has a different definition and scale to use. God, in the Old Testament, put this entire "goodness" debate to death when He said in Psalm 14:3:

> *"All have turned away, all have become corrupt; there is no one who does good, not even one."*

If no one is good, not even one, then goodness cannot be our way to heaven. God provided another way that is independent of our goodness or badness. That way is Jesus Himself. I have shared the verses in this lesson countless times to people God has brought across my path over the years. Each time I share, explain, or illustrate these basic biblical truths about Jesus and eternal life with Him, I am thankful He provided a way, in Himself, for me to live eternally with Him.

This is a bedrock, foundational truth that every growing believer in Christ needs to embrace and be able to articulate and share with conviction. I love this lesson as it shows the love of God all over again! God (essentially) threw open the doors of heaven and declared: Whoever believes in Jesus Christ will be saved! It is not just for the "good," the "church-attender," or the "perfect-has-it-all-together person"! Salvation is open, wide, and for all—through Jesus.

START HERE

 **CHAPTER 3**

Jesus Promises the Holy Spirit

The Holy Spirit* came to reside in your life the moment you placed your faith in Christ. Jesus spoke specifically about the role of the Holy Spirit in a believer's life and how He helps all believers daily as they walk with God. The Holy Spirit does not have to be a mystery! He is fully God, and He is here among us and in us. Whether you are just starting your relationship with Christ, have questions about the role of the Holy Spirit in your life, or simply want to know key passages in the Bible that point to the workings of the Holy Spirit, you are in the right place!

Passage Background

Jesus is with His disciples, sharing with them this important lesson before being put to death on the cross the next day. Again John, one of His closest disciples, records Jesus' words for scores of His followers to read and learn from in years to come. Jesus already told them He is the way to the Father, and now He comforts them with the knowledge that they will not be alone, that He will send the Holy Spirit to be with them and—better yet—to be *in* them.

John 14:16, 17

¹⁶"I will ask the Father, and He will give you another Helper, that He may be with you forever; ¹⁷that is the Spirit of truth, whom the world cannot receive, because it does not see Him or know Him, but you know Him because He abides with you and will be in you" (NASB).

John 16:7-15

⁷"But I tell you the truth, it is to your advantage that I go away; for if I do not go away, the Helper will not come to you; but if I go, I will send Him to you. ⁸And He, when He comes, will convict the world concerning sin and righteousness and judgment; ⁹concerning sin, because they do not believe in Me; ¹⁰and concerning righteousness, because I go to the Father and you no longer see Me; ¹¹and concerning judgment, because the ruler of this world has been judged.

¹²"I have many more things to say to you, but you cannot bear them now. ¹³But when He, the Spirit of truth, comes, He will guide you into all the truth; for He will not speak on His own initiative, but whatever He hears, He will speak; and He will disclose to you what is to come. ¹⁴He will glorify Me, for He will take of Mine and will disclose it to you. ¹⁵All things that the Father has are Mine; therefore I said that He takes of Mine and will disclose it to you." (NASB)

Digging Deeper

1. In John 14:16, 17, what term does Jesus use to refer to the Holy Spirit?

2. According to John 14:17, where will the Holy Spirit reside?

3. In John 16:7, who sends the Holy Spirit to us?

4. In John 16:8, what will the Holy Spirit do when He comes?

5. In John 16:13, what else will the Holy Spirit do?

You had a conscience before you placed your faith in Christ. When you placed your faith in Him, the Holy Spirit came and took residence in your heart and conscience. He guides you in small ways and big ways, from the inside out, along God's path for your life.

Just to be Clear

What pronoun is used to refer to the Holy Spirit?

Many new believers erroneously think of the Holy Spirit as an "it." Perhaps they do not understand the Holy Spirit is God. God is a person; therefore, since the Holy Spirit is part of the Trinity,* He also is a person. Jesus confirms this when He refers to the Holy Spirit as "Him."

How does it make you feel to know that Jesus did not want His followers to be alone, that He sent the Holy Spirit to be with us?

For Further Study

Read Acts 1:1-11 in your Bible.

Luke, a follower of Jesus, wrote the book of Acts, which begins where the gospels* leave off. A thrilling book to read, Acts chronicles the beginning of the church, the work of the disciples after Christ left, and how the good news* of Jesus Christ spread to other places and people groups. Acts is also a perfect place to learn more about the Holy Spirit.

1. In verses 4 and 5, what instructions did Jesus give the disciples?

2. In verse 8, what two things did Jesus say would happen when   the Holy Spirit came to the disciples?

3. What does it mean to be Jesus' witnesses?

A witness tells what he saw, heard, or experienced. Think of this in terms of a courtroom. If you testify as a witness of a car wreck, you simply take the stand and tell what you saw, heard, or experienced. Jesus asked the disciples to be His witnesses—to proclaim they saw Him die, rise again, and ascend into heaven and to tell others of His teachings, His love, and His forgiveness of sin.

Read Acts 2:1-11 in your Bible.

Pentecost was an annual festival of thanksgiving for the harvested crops. God chose this as the time and place to pour out the Holy Spirit on all those who believed in Christ.

Now when we put our faith in Christ, the Holy Spirit also is poured into our hearts and lives and fills us with God's power to overcome sin, to be His witnesses, and much more.

4. In verses 2-4, what evidence do you see that something extraordinary was taking place?

The Ongoing Role of the Holy Spirit

Read Galatians 5:16-26 in your Bible.

In this classic passage of Scripture, we learn about a battle going on in our lives daily—the battle between who we used to be before Christ came into our lives and who we are now—Christians who desire to live for God.

In your Bible, circle words and phrases that point to the Holy Spirit's leading in our lives. Depending on the version of the Bible you are using, the words may be slightly different. You may find words such as "guided by, walk with, directed by, living by, follow, live/led by, keep in step with," etc.

1. What are the things the "old you" wants to do (verses 19-21)?

2. What are the things the Holy Spirit wants to produce in your life (verse 22)?

Which fruit of the Spirit stands out to you the most? Why?

Asking to be Directed and Empowered by the Holy Spirit

Asking God to direct our life and fill us with his Holy Spirit can be a daily (even moment-by-moment) practice. Notice that the Holy Spirit never leaves us, but He may not be filling us (He may be shoved aside when we want to do things our own way). When we take control of our lives, we are in danger of missing the very best God has for us. So we can ask God to forgive us of our sins and fill us with the Holy Spirit once again.

Here is a short prayer you can pray as often as you like to continue to yield your life to God and allow the Holy Spirit to direct and empower you.

> *Dear Father, I need You. I thank You that You have forgiven my sin through Christ's death on the cross for me. Please fill me with the Holy Spirit as You commanded me to be filled and as You promised in Your Word that You would do if I asked in faith. Please produce the fruit of the Holy Spirit in my life and help me daily to say "no" to the sinful desires that tempt me. Dear Holy Spirit, please empower, direct, and fill me today."*

How easy or hard will it be for you to let the Holy Spirit direct your life?

A Few Pitfalls

From time to time some people encounter pitfalls when it comes to this topic. Two are addressed here.

1. Not Allowing the Holy Spirit to Guide Your Life

What at tragedy that Christians have the Holy Spirit in their life but do not follow His leading in their heart on a consistent basis.

The more we follow His guidance, the more we stay in step with God's plan for our lives. When He prompts you (perhaps to forgive someone, ask for forgiveness, encourage someone, say no to a destructive habit, or bless someone financially) quickly obey. God is molding you to look like the person He meant for you to be. Let Him guide and lead you and be quick to yield your will to His will—you will not regret it!

2. Not Choosing the Fruit of the Spirit

Love, peace, patience, etc., all are fruit of the Spirit as we learned earlier. The Holy Spirit wants to produce these in your life. If these wonderful attributes are not in your life and growing (bearing more fruit), explore probable reasons. You may be so used to operating one way that when the Holy Spirit wants to work on, say, being more patient, you simply lose your temper because that is what you are used to doing. When we are in bondage to sin, it is hard to choose patience. Once a person has God in her life and the Holy Spirit operating in her heart daily, she has the power to choose to operate in the fruit of the Spirit.

In Your Own Words

The new insights I learned about the Holy Spirit are …

The main message I gained from this lesson is …

This new information will affect my life in this way …

Action Steps for Next Week

○ **Prayer**: Each day ask the Holy Spirit to empower and direct your life, helping you stay in step with Christ. Consider praying a prayer thanking Jesus for the gift of the Holy Spirit.

○ **Bible**: Continue reading in the Gospel of John. This week read chapters 5-8. Use a highlighter as you read and highlight verses that stand out to you, encourage you, or raise questions.

○ **Attend**: Attend a small-group Bible study. This may be at a church on a Sunday morning (typically called "Sunday school") or through a Christian ministry during the week. Getting connected to a group of other believers will be paramount to your growing walk with God.

○ **Others**: Pray and ask God if there is a friend or family member you can invite to join you for church or some other Christian gathering.

When the Holy Spirit nudges at your heart to talk to someone about Christ or to invite that person to church with you, He is helping you, directing you, and empowering you to be His witness.

○ **Memorize**: Recite John 14:16. Also review the past weeks' verses. Memorizing one verse a week is a common practice among Christians. Memorized verses will help you when God brings opportunities to witness for Him. Even if you do not have your Bible with you, you will be able to share truth about God, Jesus, and the Holy Spirit.

Prayer Journal

This space can be used to write a prayer to God, to record items you are praying about and the date they are answered, or to keep track of others you want to pray for.

_____

_____

_____

_____

_____

_____

_____

_____

Personally Speaking

Wow, that was a long chapter! There is so much to learn about the Holy Spirit, and I did not want to leave any key pieces out. How precious that Jesus did not leave us alone. The Holy Spirit came to be with us and in us.

I distinctly remember having an "A-ha" moment when I learned the Holy Spirit was real—not a mist or a ghost or a great idea, but real. He was God and real in my heart, directing me. I also remember learning the Holy Spirit is a "He" not an "it." One cannot really have a meaningful love relationship with an "it." Sadly, I do not think I really grasped this for about four years after I became a Christian.

Ephesians 1:13 says: "And you also were included in Christ when you heard the message of truth, the gospel of your salvation. When you believed, you were marked in Him with a seal, the promised Holy Spirit, who is a deposit guaranteeing our inheritance until the redemption of those who are God's possession—to the praise of His glory."

This verse holds special meaning to me as it shows how, the moment I believed in Christ, I was marked with the seal of the Holy Spirit. He is my guarantee that I am a child of God, that I am secure in Christ, and that there is more to come! Similar to an engagement ring, the Holy Spirit residing in me is a guarantee that there is more yet to come in my life, walk, and eternity with God.

Practically each morning before my feet hit the floor, I begin praying. I pray prayers of thankfulness, prayers for people God brings to mind. My main prayer, however, is asking the Holy Spirit to fill me, empower me, and direct me through the day.

I often pray, "Dear Holy Spirit, please fill me to over flowing to touch nations." As I pray I have this picture in my mind that the Holy Spirit so fills and overflows out of me, the ripple effect flows even to people in other nations.

I am so thankful for Holy Spirit's role in my life. He has sealed me, matured me, convicted me, illuminated Scripture, and prompted me to step out in faith hundreds of times. Oh, how I love Him!

 **CHAPTER 4**

Jesus Teaches About Prayer

Jesus prayed. He prayed for Himself, His disciples, and for future believers. He also taught about prayer. Prayer is our way of communicating with God whenever we want and wherever we are, whether out loud or in our hearts. Learning more about prayer, what to pray for, and key Bible passages that teach about prayer is a great foundation for our growing relationship with God.

Passage Background

Jesus prayed at each significant event in His life and ministry. He prayed when He was baptized* (Mark 1:21), when He selected His disciples (Luke 6:12-16), in the upper room after the Last Supper (John 17:1-26), in the garden of Gethsemane before His crucifixion (Luke 22:41, 42), and even on the cross before He died (Luke 23: 34). He prayed alone and with others. This constant example of prayer prompted His disciples to ask further about how to pray. Jesus readily taught them how to pray and even gave them an example of a prayer to use that serves as our example as well.

Luke 11:1-4

[1]"Now it came to pass, as He was praying in a certain place, when He ceased, that one of His disciples said to Him, 'Lord, teach us to pray, as John also taught his disciples.' [2]So He said to them, 'When you pray, say:

> *Our Father in heaven,*
> *Hallowed be Your name.*
> *Your kingdom come.*
> *Your will be done*
> *On earth as it is in heaven.*
> [3]*Give us day by day our daily bread.*
> [4]*And forgive us our sins,*
> *For we also forgive everyone who is indebted to us.*
> *And do not lead us into temptation,*
> *But deliver us from the evil one.'"*

(New King James Version)

Digging Deeper

1. "Father" was a common way Jesus referred to His relationship with God the Father while He was on earth. He prompted His disciples to refer to God the Father that way as well.

How does it make you feel that God wants you to address him as "Father"?

2. This prayer begins with acknowledging who God is, acknowledging He has a kingdom, and acknowledging we desire His will to be done.

Why do you think it is important to begin our prayers with this in mind?

How difficult or easy is it for you to ask for God's will to be done in your life?

3. According to this prayer, what are some things we can ask God for?

4. Forgiveness of sins is a key part of this prayer. Why do you think it is important to ask God to forgive our sins? Why should we also forgive others when they sin against us?

Just to be Clear

1. Does this passage mention a certain time of day you need to pray?

2. Does this passage mention a certain place you need to be when you pray?

3. Does this passage mention a certain position you need to be in to pray?

You do not have to pray every morning, every night, or follow some other rule for prayer you may give yourself. Faith in God is a relationship.

What would you think of a parent who said to her children, "You can talk to me at 7:00 a.m., at meal times, and then before you go to bed." How rigid and mean that would be! That is not what a relationship is about.

You may find a time of day to specifically set aside to pray and read Scripture, but communication with God also can be an all-day conversation. There is no certain place you need to be to talk to God; He is everywhere, and the Holy Spirit is in your life (as we learned in the last lesson). You can pray in your kitchen, in church, at your job, or with a friend—your options are limitless! Further, a person does not need to be on her knees, head bowed, or eyes closed. Many Christians pray in their cars while driving, so there is no way to get into a certain position to pray!

For Further Study

Read John 17:1-26 in your Bible.

This entire chapter is Jesus' prayer the night before He is taken to the cross and crucified.

1. In verses 1-5, Jesus is praying for Himself.

    o   In verse 4, how did Jesus bring glory to God?

    o   In verse 5, what time period does Jesus refer to?

Jesus came to earth for a specific task: to die as the perfect sacrifice for all mankind—once and for all—to pay the penalty for sin.

In this verse Jesus asks the Father to restore Him, after His resurrection, to the rightful place of glory He always had before the world even began.

2. In verses 6-18 Jesus prays for His disciples.

o Circle in your Bible words that show how Jesus asks God to protect us. Depending on the version of the Bible you use, the words may be slightly different. You may find words such as "keep them in Your care, keep/kept, guard/guarded, keep safe, protect/protected."

o Who does Jesus say He is protecting us from (verse 15)?

Unfortunately we have a foe. The evil one, Satan*, hates God and hates Christians. He is against us and everything we try to do for God. He is out to destroy us, discourage us, and make us useless in God's kingdom. So another item we can pray for is protection for ourselves and protection against any distractions or temptations the devil may throw our way.

3. In verses 20-26, Jesus prays for future believers.

o In verse 20, who is Jesus praying for?

o How does it make you feel that Jesus prayed for you while on earth?

A Few Pitfalls

From time to time some people encounter pitfalls when it comes to this topic. Five are addressed here.

1. **Using Eloquent Language or Strange Words in Prayer**

   Prayer is simply talking to God. You do not need to use any words not used in your own daily life and language. There is no right or wrong way to pray; God already knows your heart, so do not sweat the wording.

2. **Using Repetitive Words in Prayer**

   Repeating the same words over and over (even God's name) does not make your prayers any more powerful than just simply talking to God, praising Him, and asking for your needs

3. **Saying the Same Scripted Prayer Repeatedly Each Day**

   Prayer is not a magic formula; it needs to be personal. Your heart has to be in your prayers. It is not so much the words as it is the attitude of your heart, so prayer does not need to be ritualistic. Personal, real and honest prayer is best.

4. **Thinking God Does Not Want to be Bothered by Your Prayers**

   Not true! You can pray to God about anything and everything, big or small. God loves you and is concerned about the details of your life. So pray about everything; God loves your communication with Him.

5. Not Realizing How Unforgiveness Is a Pitfall to Prayer

In His prayer, Jesus modeled asking God to forgive us and us to forgive others. When we do not forgive others who have wronged or hurt us, it is hypocritical for us to ask God to forgive us our sins against Him. So forgive others in your heart, just as you want God to forgive you.

Which one of these pitfalls have you fallen into in the past?

Do you think there are other prayer pitfalls people fall into?

In Your Own Words

The new insights I learned about prayer are ...

The main message I gained from this lesson is ...

This new information will affect my life in this way ...

Action Steps for Next Week

o **Prayer**: Consider praying to God a prayer of thankfulness that you can talk to Him anytime, anywhere. Share with Him your praise, hopes, fears, and needs.

o   **Bible**: Continue reading the Gospel of John. Read chapters 9-12 this week. If you have questions about what you are reading, consider asking a trusted Christian friend, a woman discipling you, or a minister at your church.

o   **Discipleship**: Many Christian organizations and churches offer discipleship. Consider asking someone in your church/small group if she will help you locate a person to disciple you—someone who has been a Christian for a longer period of time who will meet regularly with you to help you grow deeper in your relationship with God.

o   **Others**: Pray for someone in your life who needs a special touch or help from God. You may wish to tell the person of your prayers and ask for specific prayer requests.

o   **Forgiveness**: This lesson also briefly talked about forgiveness. Do you need to ask God's forgiveness for anything? Is there anyone you need to ask to forgive you? Is there anyone you need to forgive?

o   **Memorize**: Recite Luke 11:1-4. Review past Scripture verses you have memorized.

Prayer Journal

This space can be used write a prayer to God, to record items you are praying about and the date they are answered, or to keep track of others you want to pray for.

_____
_____
_____
_____
_____
_____
_____
_____

Personally Speaking

I remember praying as a young child. My mother taught me to pray the Lord's Prayer, and I recited it each night at bedtime. She also taught me to say a blessing for my food at mealtimes. I remember praying for God to help me each morning in elementary school when the principal of my school took a moment of silence in our morning announcements.

As I grew into a teenager, my life became consumed with trying to please my peers through wild living. During that phase of my life, I used prayer like a vacuum cleaner. When I created some type of mess in my life though poor choices, I desperately prayed for God to clean it up. When He did, I simply put the vacuum back up until I created another mess.

At the age of 16, after learning of God's love for me and my sinfulness, I knelt beside a pew in church and put my faith and trust in Jesus Christ. That prayer of salvation was sincere, from the heart, and life-changing.

I have always loved the words God spoke through the prophet Jeremiah to the Israelite people. In this verse God beckons them, and now us, to come to Him in prayer.

> *"For I know the plans I have for you," declares the* LORD, *plans to prosper you and not to harm you, plans to give you hope and a future. Then you will call on me and come and pray to me, and I will listen to you" (Jeremiah 29:11).*

Communicating with God through prayer is such a gift. We, mere humans with finite brains, can approach God Almighty on His throne and bring Him our thoughts, praises, requests, hurts, excitements, and adoration—and He says He will listen! What a joy! How thankful I am God has thrown open the doors of heaven and beckoned us to come to Him in prayer.

 **CHAPTER 5**

Jesus Uses Scripture

Knowing God's Word, the Bible, is paramount for any Christian desiring to grow deeper in her relationship with Christ. God's Word helps followers of Christ make wise decisions, encourages them when they are fearful, uplifts them when they are broken-hearted, and convicts them when they stray. In this lesson we will dig deeper into understanding God's Word and how He uses it to help us in our lives. We also will look at some practical information about how the Bible came to be and why it can be trusted.

Passage Background

John the Baptist, the cousin of Jesus, baptized* Him in the Jordan River. John lived his life preparing others for the coming of Christ. Jesus asked John to baptize Him, and after Jesus came out of the water, John saw the Spirit of God descend on Jesus like a dove. He heard God say, "This is My beloved Son, in whom I am well-pleased" (Matthew 3:17, NASB). It was after this baptism* that Jesus went into the wilderness where Satan tempted Him.

Matthew 4:1-11

¹"Then Jesus was led by the Spirit into the wilderness to be tempted by the devil. ²After fasting forty days and forty nights, He was hungry. ³The tempter came to Him and said, 'If you are the Son of God, tell these stones to become bread.' ⁴Jesus answered, 'It is written: "Man shall not live on bread alone, but on every word that comes from the mouth of God." ⁵Then the devil took Him to the holy city and had Him stand on the highest point of the temple. ⁶'If You are the Son of God,' he said, 'throw Yourself down. For it is written: "He will command His angels concerning You, and they will lift You up in their hands, so that You will not strike Your foot against a stone." ⁷Jesus answered him, 'It is also written: "Do not put the Lord your God to the test." ⁸Again, the devil took Him to a very high mountain and showed Him all the kingdoms of the world and their splendor. 'All this I will give You,' he said, 'if You will bow down and worship me.' ¹⁰Jesus said to him, 'Away from Me, Satan! For it is written: "Worship the Lord your God, and serve Him only." ¹¹Then the devil left Him, and angels came and attended Him."

Digging Deeper

1. What did Jesus say as a response to Satan each time Satan tempted Him?

2. Why do you think Satan tempted Jesus to turn stones into bread?

3. Satan used Scripture to tempt Jesus. According to this passage, does Satan know Scripture?

What is the difference between how Satan used Scripture and how Jesus used Scripture?

4. When Satan showed Jesus all the kingdoms of the world, what did Satan want Jesus to do?

The way Jesus used Scripture from the Old Testament to combat the temptations of Satan is an incredible example of how we can use Scripture as well. Satan tempted Jesus to stray from the very reason He was sent to earth—to die on the cross for our sins—by asking Jesus to bow down to him and worship him. Jesus did not argue with him, He simply used Scripture to stay in step with God's plan. Satan will do anything he can to tempt us, discourage us, and confuse us—even using Scripture to do it! Jesus' responses demonstrate that God's Word is powerful, alive, and withstands the test of time.

For Further Study

Read 2 Timothy 3:16, 17 in your Bible.

"God-breathed" (or your Bible may say "inspired") gives us the mental picture of God breathing His life into the writings of the biblical authors. The Spirit of God moved them to write what they did, and the result is exactly what God intended.

1. What does verse 16 say Scripture is useful for?

2. How do you think the Bible corrects us (verse 16)?

3. How do you think the Bible equips us for every good work (verse 17)?

How the Bible (Canon) Came Together

"The term 'canon' is used to describe the books that are divinely inspired and therefore belong in the Bible. Determining the canon was a process conducted first by Jewish rabbis and scholars and later by early Christians. Ultimately, it was God who decided what books belonged in the biblical canon. A book of Scripture belonged in the canon from the moment God inspired its writing. It was simply a matter of God's convincing His human followers which books should be included in the Bible." — CEO, S. Michael Houdmann of GotQuestions.org

For more on this please refer to the "Answers and Explanations" section.

Why We Can Trust the Bible

The Bible has been tested, scrutinized, and debated and has stood the test of time. The Bible is different from all other human writings in its continuity, circulation, and survival. The list below contains a few of the ways we can know that what we read in the Bible can be trusted as the Word of God.

o *Internal Evidence*: This type of evidence determines the credibility of the written record by analyzing the ability of the writer or the witness to tell the truth.

   Throughout the New Testament, the writers often refer to what they had seen or heard. Many of their contemporaries also had witnessed Jesus' life.

   If the writers had reported facts incorrectly, those contemporaries could have challenged their writing.

The disciples had to be careful to write down events just as they had happened.

Another reason we can trust the reliability of the New Testament and the authors' records about Jesus' life is because the authors willingly recorded incidents that portrayed themselves in a negative light. Examples include the disciples' flight after Jesus' arrest and their competition for a high place in God's kingdom. The Bible also is internally consistent. This means there are no contradictions between books and authors. Given these facts, we can trust the New Testament's portrayal of Christ.

o **External Evidence**: Historians use this type of evidence to verify the reliability of a document. They look for evidence of biblical places, people, and events confirmed outside of the pages of the Bible. Historians and archaeologists have confirmed the events, timelines, and people in the Bible through outside documents and historical records.

Even ancient, unbelieving historians wrote about Jesus, His followers, and the government during the time of Christ. They confirm many of the major events in the New Testament. Lee Strobel in his book, *The Case for Christ*, cites the following example of external evidence.

"The Gospel of John tells of Jesus healing a cripple next to the Pool of Bethesda. The text even describes the five porticoes (walkways) leading to the pool.

Scholars didn't think the pool existed, until archaeologists found it forty feet below ground, complete with the five porticoes." Strobel, Lee, *The Case for Christ* (Zondervan Publishing House, 1998), p. 132.

o **Prophetic Evidence**: This evidence explores prophecies about the Messiah and if/when they were fulfilled.

o   The Old Testament contains more than 300 prophecies of the coming Messiah that were fulfilled in Jesus.

The fulfillment of these prophecies points to the reliability of the other information presented in the Old and New Testaments.

A few examples of Old Testament prophecies and their fulfillment:

o   The Messiah will be born in Bethlehem (Micah 5:2).

o   He will come out of Egypt (Hosea 11:1).

Jesus fulfilled each of these prophecies.

o   He was born in Bethlehem (Matthew 2: 1).

o   His parents took Him to Egypt to escape Herod's order to kill all boys two years old and younger (Matthew 2: 13, 14).

How does it make you feel that God wanted to be known by you and so preserved His Word so you could read it, study it, and know Him?

Does reading information like this about the Bible increase your confidence that you can trust it? Why or why not?

A Few Pitfalls

From time to time, some people encounter pitfalls when it comes to this topic.

Three are addressed here.

1. **Since the Bible has been translated so many times, how do I know that the copy I have is trustworthy?**

    Some people erroneously claim that since the Bible has been translated so many times, it has errors. The fact is, though, translators use the most dependable manuscripts written in the original language that are available today.

    This means today's translators use original Greek, Hebrew, and Aramaic source texts to translate the Bible into modern languages.

2. **The Bible is such a big book, I don't know where to start; I am overwhelmed by it.**

    The Bible is a big book broken down into two main parts: the Old Testament (written before Christ) and the New Testament (written after Christ). It further breaks down into 66 separate books. Any great undertaking starts with a first step. Consider beginning to read the Bible by starting with the Gospel of John. Read a few verses each day. Additionally, consider investing in a Bible commentary.

    A commentary will help you understand what you read by giving definitions of words, illustrations, and further information about the verses.

3. **I am too busy to read the Bible.**

    The Bible is the primary way you will come to know God and His heart, love, and purpose for you. Think about this in the context of a relationship.

    If you love someone, or are falling in love with someone, you would make time to be with that person to learn about him, and you would talk to him.

In the same way, in the midst of our busy lives, carving out time with God helps all the busyness fall into place.

Spending time with God will help your life line up with His purposes for you—and that is worth making time for.

Which one of the pitfalls stands out to you the most?

Do you think there are other pitfalls not listed here?

In Your Own Words

The new insights I learned about God's Word are …

The main message I gained from this lesson is …

This new information will affect my life in this way …

Action Steps for Next Week

o **Prayer**: Thank God in prayer for His Word that not only is trustworthy, but also reveals who He is and how you can know Him more deeply.

o **Bible**: Continue reading the Gospel of John. Read chapters 13-16 this week. You are almost done!

o **Plugging In**: Move from merely attending a church to looking for opportunities to "plug in" and perhaps serve— such as bringing food for an outreach, helping to organize a women's retreat, working with children, etc.

God gives each person gifts and special abilities. Those gifts and abilities can be used mightily in the church to help others.

o **Others**: Is there a Scripture you like or one that has been an encouragement to you thus far in this study? Look for opportunities to share it with someone this week to encourage him or her.

o **Memorize**: Recite Matthew 4:4. Review past verses you have memorized.

Prayer Journal

This space can be used to write a prayer to God, to record items you are praying about and the date they are answered, or to keep track of others you want to pray for.

_____
_____
_____
_____
_____
_____
_____

Personally Speaking

There have been different seasons in my life when the only way I believe I made it through was to hang onto a particular Scripture from God's Word. I recited a verse that encouraged me each time I wanted to crumble in fear.

For example, I went through a period in college when I was very fearful of someone (father, mother, sister) dying. While walking across campus, if the thought came to mind of one of them dying, I would be in tears by the time I reached my classroom. I felt compelled to think through how I would manage without them, their funerals, and how sad I would be. I would think about the loss I would feel later in life without them at different milestones of my life. Then I would remember and recite Scripture such as, "For God has not given us a spirit of fear and timidity, but of power, love, and self-discipline" (2 Timothy 1:7, NLT). I recited it over and over and reminded myself that this fear of the worst happening was not coming from God. I did not need to let fear steal my joy of that day.

When I was older and crushed in spirit when another potential marriage relationship dissolved, I would cling to Psalm 34:18, "The Lord is close to the brokenhearted and saves those who are crushed in spirit."

When I prayed again and again for many, many years for my father to trust Christ as his Lord and Savior, I often recited 2 Peter 3:9, "The Lord is not slow in keeping His promise, as some understand slowness. Instead He is patient with you, not wanting anyone to perish, but everyone to come to repentance." God is patient. My father did not trust Christ until the age of 50!

I encourage you to read God's Word each day. Discover for yourself what God may be saying to you through the Bible.

Additionally, your local Christian bookstore offers books that group verses of Scripture together according to topic.

For example if you wanted to find numerous Scriptures dealing with worry, doubt, fear, weariness, etc., you simply turn to the chapter covering that topic, and dozens of verses would be listed there for you.

Reading God's Word daily, relying on His wisdom from Scripture to make decisions, and learning how He wants me to see Him and relate to Him based on Scripture has shaped and molded who I am. I love studying God's Word, for it is new, fresh, and alive each day! There always is a new lesson God has for me to learn, to apply to my life, and to be encouraged by.

START HERE

 **CHAPTER 6**

Jesus Gives the Great Commission

Upon His leaving, Jesus gave specific instructions to His disciples, and those same directions have been given to you and me as well. Jesus has given us a purpose in life: to know Him and to make Him known to others. These instructions are known as the Great Commission. He commissioned His disciples—and you and me— to go and share what we have learned.

Passage Background

Matthew, a Jewish tax collector who became one of Jesus' disciples, wrote the Gospel of Matthew. He wrote this account of Jesus' life specifically to the Jewish people to present clear evidence that Jesus was the long-awaited Messiah. The verses we will study are the final verses in the Gospel of Matthew. Here Jesus speaks His last words to His disciples, and soon afterward He ascended into heaven.

Matthew 28:18-20

¹⁸"Jesus came and told His disciples, 'I have been given all authority in heaven and on earth. ¹⁹Therefore, go and make disciples of all the nations, baptizing them in the name of the Father and the Son and the Holy Spirit. ²⁰Teach these new disciples to obey all the commands I have given you. And be sure of this: I am with you always, even to the end of the age'" (NLT).

Digging Deeper

1. What did Jesus tell His disciples to do in verses 19 and 20?

2. What does Jesus assure them of in verse 20?

How do you think Jesus is with us?

For Further Study

Read Mark 16:15, 16 in your Bible.

1. Compare these verses with the verses from Matthew. List any similarities.

2. Compare the verses again and list any differences.

Based on these verses, what do you conclude Jesus wanted His followers then (and now) to do?

Just to be Clear

1. In the first passage, is making disciples a mere suggestion?

2. Is there any reference in these passages about needing to be a pastor or a vocational missionary or needing a theology degree to tell others about Christ?

3. Is there any reference to keeping silent and hoping someone will ask us about our faith in Jesus?

Jesus gave clear and bold instructions when He commissioned all His followers to continue what He started and spread the good news to all nations. We are to be a part of the Great Commission by going to the nations, giving to endeavors that spread the gospel to the nations, and using our talents, gifts, and time to this purpose.

A Few Simple Steps to Sharing Your Faith and Discipling Others

o   ***Pray*** for God to open your eyes to people around you who might not know Him or have a personal relationship with Him. These might be people in your family or neighborhood, co-workers or friends.

o **Look** for ways to care for people and show the love of Christ in action, such as taking a meal to someone who is sick, caring for a friend's child, or helping a co-worker.

o **Tell** a person, "Sometime I would love to hear about your spiritual journey." If you sense he or she is open to talking more, set up a time to listen to his or her journey and perhaps share the gospel* message and your testimony.* Share the simple prayer and decision you made to put your faith in Christ and ask if he or she would like to do the same.

o **Offer** to pray for a person, bring that person to church, and invite him or her to Christian gatherings such as a Bible study or social get-together.

o **Realize** it may take a day or years for a person to trust Christ. Do not pressure anyone, just simply look for opportunities to pray for people, care for them, show the love of God, and share your story when you can.

o **Disciple others** by simply teaching them what you have been taught or what you have learned as you have grown in your relationship with God. You can meet with someone weekly or bi-weekly. You can use this book as the content for your first six meetings.

Which one of the steps listed above would be easiest for you?

Which one would be the most challenging to you?

Can you identify some communities where God has placed you to be a witness for Him (office, dorm, neighborhood, etc.)? List them here.

You soon will find that being a part of the Great Commission and following Jesus' instructions to preach the good news and make disciples is one of the most thrilling parts to being a follower of Christ!

A Few Pitfalls

From time to time some people encounter pitfalls when it comes to this topic. Three are addressed here.

1. **Erroneously believing you have to know a lot before you tell others about Christ.**

   Not so. You do not have to know all the answers or have read the entire Bible or be an expert in the things of God. Simply tell your story—how you first heard about Christ, what your life was like before you chose to follow Him, how you put your faith in Him, and the difference He has made in your life since. If someone asks a difficult question, it is perfectly fine to say, "I don't know the answer to that question, but I will research it and get back with you."

2. **Leaving the Great Commission work to professional career missionaries.**

   We all are missionaries in the sense that our mission field is where God has put us right now. Your mission field may be your dorm floor, your children's play group, your workplace, or your family. Each of those is a mission field where God can use you to reach people for Him and thus help fulfill the Great Commission.

While it is true that some people pursue full-time career mission work, we all are a part of the Great Commission. These instructions were given for all Christ's followers.

3. **Wondering if your salvation story is dramatic enough to share with others.**

   Whether you trusted Christ when young or old, as a well-behaved kid or a wild teenager, in church or at home, the fact that the God of the universe came into your life when you put your faith in Him is amazing and dramatic!

   Do not discount your salvation story because it might not sound like another person's story.

Which one of these pitfalls stands out to you the most?

Is there another pitfall you can think of not listed here?

In Your Own Words

The new insights I learned about the Great Commission are ...

The main message I gained from this lesson is ...

This new information will affect my life in this way ...

Action Steps for Next Week

o **Prayer**: Pray and ask God to help you advance the Great Commission in your lifetime. Ask Him to help you be a bold witness for Him in each community you are a part of.

o **Bible**: Finish reading the Gospel of John, chapters 17-21. Fantastic! The Bible consists of 66 books, and you have read one of them! Which will be your next?

o **Baptism**: Baptism is mentioned in the key passage of this chapter. Baptism is when a person publically professes what has taken place in her heart. Through the act of baptism, she proclaims her trust in Christ for the forgiveness of her sins and her desire for Him to be Lord of her life. Most baptisms take place during church services. Consider being baptized at the church you attend.

o **Others**: Consider discipling someone. Invite a person to meet regularly for prayer, encouragement, and Bible study. Perhaps study this book together, and share with her the things you learned about Christ the first time you went through it. Who will you ask to meet with you?

o **Memorize**: Recite Matthew 28:18-20 each day for a week. Review past verses. Once a week, recite these six verses to keep them fresh in your mind. What verse do you want to memorize next?

Prayer Journal

This space can be used to write a prayer to God, to record items you are praying about and the date they are answered, or to keep track of others you want to pray for.

_____

_____

_____

_____

_____

_____

_____

_____

Personally Speaking

I remember years ago writing a life mission statement that was based, in part, on Matthew 28:18-20. It read: _My life mission statement is to fall deeper in love with God and to tell others about Him._

Although simple, it has guided me in many decisions, large and small, over the years. For example, if I started sleeping through my designated time with God, or spending that time checking my email, or just letting the busyness of life squeeze that time out, I would say to myself, "Lori, you wanted your life to be about falling deeper in love with God. Email and busyness are not going to help that happen. Spending time in God's Word will." Or when deciding whether or not to go on a particular mission trip, to take on a new role at work, to volunteer in my neighborhood, or even to write books, I would ask myself, "Will this help tell others about Him or not?"

So for me, having an overarching purpose in life has helped to give me focus and to make decisions through the different stages of my life. That overarching purpose is God's purpose: the Great Commission.

I want to add to His mighty, everlasting kingdom, not build my own little kingdom on earth. His kingdom will last; mine will fade as soon as the last folks who personally know me die. Keeping my mind and heart focused on an eternal perspective helps me to this end. These are a few verses I use to meditate on my life, the real end goal of life, and all humanity.

"And this gospel of the kingdom will be preached in the whole world as a testimony to all nations, and then the end will come" (Matthew 24:14).

"After this I looked, and there before me was a great multitude that no one could count, from every nation, tribe, people and language, standing before the throne and before the Lamb. They were wearing white robes and were holding palm branches in their hands. And they cried out in a loud voice: "Salvation belongs to our God, who sits on the throne, and to the Lamb"(Revelation 7:9-10).

"Look, I am coming soon! My reward is with Me, and I will give to each person according to what they have done. I am the Alpha and the Omega, the First and the Last, the Beginning and the End" (Revelation 22:12-13).

Meditating about the gospel going forth to all nations and Jesus returning helps me focus on Him and His kingdom instead of getting caught up in trivial, smaller, petty issues that will not matter long term. Keeping Him and His plan before me becomes my anchor, my north star, my map to life! May it be to you as well. Praise be to God!

START HERE

Glossary of Helpful Terms

Apostle: "Sent one," a messenger or missionary. This word became the official title for Jesus' twelve disciples after His death and resurrection.

Baptize/Baptized/Baptism: A public proclamation of the fact that one has put one's trust in Jesus Christ and His payment for sins through His death on the cross. It is an outward symbol of what already has taken place in the heart—that of trusting Christ to forgive one's sins and give the gift of eternal life with Him.

Disciple: A learner or follower. Jesus chose twelve men/disciples to learn from Him and follow Him during His earthly ministry. Anyone can follow Christ and learn from Christ. The first step is to put one's faith in Him. If you are helping another woman learn and grow in her relationship with Christ, she can be called your disciple. The expression "She discipled me when I was in college" refers to someone being helped in her walk with God on a consistent basis by another Christian.

Discipler: The leader or teacher in a discipling relationship, responsible for loving, encouraging, and patiently walking alongside another in his or her spiritual growth.

God: Also called "Father." He created all creation as outlined in Genesis (the first book of the Bible).

Good news: Another word for gospel. If someone says, "A woman shared the good news with me, and I have never been the same," it means someone shared the gospel message of salvation in Christ with that person.

Gospel: Refers to the message of salvation in Christ. Example: Yesterday I shared the gospel with my friend. Also the proper name of the first four books of the New Testament, e.g., the Gospel of John. Also commonly used to refer to music with Christian themes. For example: I love listening to gospel music.

Heaven: The home of God and His angels. Those who have placed their faith in Christ will one day be there with God. Jesus now is in heaven and lives to make intercession for us as believers.

Holy Spirit: Also referred to as the Holy Ghost, the Spirit, and Helper. He is not a literal ghost, but rather the third person of the Godhead, or Trinity, God the Holy Spirit. When a person places his or her faith in Jesus Christ as Savior and Lord, the Holy Spirit comes to reside in that new believer's heart.

Jesus: Also called "Christ" or "Lord Jesus." He is God and came down from heaven and became a man. He was fully God and fully man. He died and paid the penalty for our sins. On earth He commonly referred to God as "Father."

New Testament: The books of the Bible written after Christ died and rose again. This includes the four Gospels, the book of Acts that chronicles the growth of the early church and the spread of the gospel, and many letters written by disciples and apostles (even one by Jesus' half-brother, James). These books and letters were compiled and labeled the New Testament.

Old Testament: The books of the Bible written before Christ. It starts in Genesis, describing how God created the earth, the first man and woman, and all living things. Books chronicling the history of the nation of Israel, books of poetry, and books of prophecy complete the Old Testament. Prophecies concerning the coming Messiah, Jesus Christ, are woven throughout these books.

Satan: Also called devil and Evil One, an angel who desired to be higher than God. He and the angels that sided with him in heaven were cast out of heaven. He is described in Scripture as a liar, a tempter, and is the enemy of our faith.

Scripture: Any word, verse, or passage found in the Bible. The Bible also is called "God's Word."

Testimony: Your story of how and when you placed your faith in Jesus Christ.

Trinity: Christians use this term to describe the three-in-one nature of God: God the Father, God the Son, and God the Holy Spirit. Examples of God being three in one are throughout the Bible. I have listed two here.

- o   In John 14:16, all three Persons of the Trinity are mentioned: I (Jesus), Father, Helper (the Holy Spirit).

"I will ask the Father, and He will give you another Helper, that He may be with you forever" (NASB).

- o   In Matthew 28:19 all three Persons of the Trinity are mentioned.

"Therefore, go and make disciples of all nations, baptizing them in the name of the Father and the Son and of the Holy Spirit."

Note that the text says the name of the Father, Son and the Holy Spirit—not the names.

There are many ways people have sought to describe the Trinity. This picture of a triangle with three corners is my favorite illustration. Notice that all three corners are equal. No matter how you would turn the triangle it would still be one triangle. In the same way, God is one God with three distinct roles.

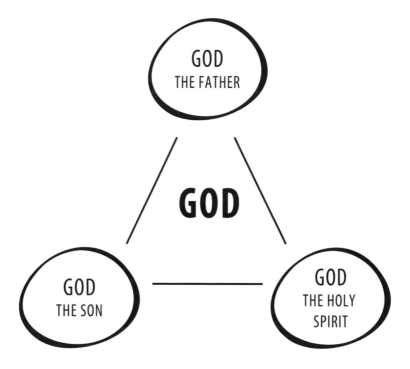

Answers and Explanations

Chapter 1: Jesus Demonstrates God's Love

Digging Deeper

1. According to verse 16, what happens to people who believe in Jesus? (We have eternal life.) Perishing is what happens to those who do not believe in Jesus—in this context it means living eternally without God in hell (because of our sin and not placing our faith in Christ).

2. According to verse 17, why did God send Jesus to earth? (To save the world.)

3. In verse 16, Jesus talks about eternal life. Find John 17:3 in your Bible. How does that verse define eternal life? (Life with God now and forever.)

Just to be Clear

This section addresses the fact that sometimes we attach meanings, ideas, or thoughts to God that are not in Scripture.

Perhaps we have been taught this erroneously or picked this up somewhere along the way and internalized it. The "Just to be Clear" section seeks to shave off teachings inconsistent with what God teaches us in His Word.

1. According to verse 16, who loved first, us or God? (God.) God loved the world first. He decided to create it and man and woman out of love. He loved us first. Even when we were/are sinners, He loves us. Before we were born, He loved.

2. According to verse 17, did Jesus come to judge/condemn the world? (No.) He came to help, to save, to forgive, and to show God's love. Sadly many outside of the Christian faith think the opposite, but when you look at Jesus' words and actions while on earth, they clearly show He was here to save and help.

For Further Study

1. According to verse 9, how do we know Jesus loves us? (He said it.) He demonstrated it by laying down His life as a sacrifice for ours.

2. According to verse 10, how do we show our love for God? (By obeying His commands.) God gave us commands to help us live in peace with people and Him. As you read the Bible, you will come across these commands, and I encourage you to highlight them.

Commands such as not stealing, lying or committing adultery (Exodus 20) and commands against hatred, rage, and selfishness (Galatians 5) are just a few.

3. According to verse 12, what is Jesus' commandment to us in this passage? (Love each other.) Jesus wants us to love others as He has loved us. He loved us when we were selfish, sinful, and many times going down our own path to our detriment! I can say that loving people seems easy at first. Wow, what an easy commandment, right? People can be hard to love. I pray for God to give me His love for others, His heart for others, and the ability to see people the way He does.

4. According to verse 13, what is the greatest way to show your love for another? (To die for that person.) God loved us and demonstrated this love by sending His son to die as our substitute, in our place. We deserved punishment for our sins, but Jesus bore it for us on the cross.

A Few Pitfalls

1. A Wrong View of God

I talk about this subject at length in my first book *Discipling Women*. Identifying lies you may believe about God and replacing them with truth from God's Word is paramount to further growth in Christ. Two books I have read on this subject are *God: Discover His Character* by Bill Bright and *Praying the Names of God* by Ann Spangler.

2. **Lack of Reading Scripture to Learn More About God**
    Recently, I began setting my clock to get up before my children, and I spend time reading the Bible and praying during the quietness of the morning. Even though I feel very tired when that alarm goes off, I always am glad that I spent time with God and gave Him the first of my day.

Chapter 2: Jesus Is the Way to the Father

Digging Deeper

1. In verse 1, who does Jesus want us to trust? (God and Him.)

2. In verse 6, how does Jesus say a person comes to the Father? (Through Him.) Jesus is making it as clear as possible for people to grasp that salvation is found in Him alone, not in another religion, not in being good, nor in anything else we may look to for eternal life.

Just to be Clear

In John 14:6, did Jesus open the door for other ways that can lead to God? (No.) In this verse Jesus says the way to the Father is through Him. He left no door open for there to be any other way to eternal life with God than through a personal relationship with Him.

For Further Study

1. Grace means unmerited favor or an undeserved gift. How is a relationship with Jesus an underserved gift? (We did nothing to deserve it.) Grace is a free gift. I remember in college I was studying feverishly for a test I was not prepared for. Upon walking into the class, the professor decided to give the class a "grace period," and he postponed the test until the following week. I was elated!

I did not deserve the grace period, but took the extra days to study. That is grace, a free gift.

That is what God extends to us through Christ: grace. Jesus was our substitute. He took on the punishment we earned with our sins. We broke God's commandments (and still do), and yet God put Christ to death—not us! So our forgiveness and relationship with Christ are gifts. We did not earn them. God gave them.

2. Saved is a term used to describe a person who has a personal relationship with Jesus. By placing our trust in Jesus Christ, we are saved from hell. According to this verse how are we saved? (By placing our faith in Jesus Christ.) When a person places her faith in Jesus Christ, she trusts that when He died on the cross He was doing it for her. He lived a sinless life and took on the punishment we deserved for our sins. Putting our faith and trust in Him and His death saves us from hell.

3. Faith means to believe in or trust in someone or something. Who are we to have faith in? (Jesus.)

4. Works means good things done hoping to earn God's favor. According to this verse, is salvation based on good works? (No.)

What are good works some people may try to rely on to be saved? (Giving to charity, volunteering, giving money to homeless, community service, going to church, etc.) We need only to rely on Jesus, not on ourselves and the good things we can do, for salvation. If we rely on ourselves, we may frequently wonder if we did enough to attain heaven.

If we rely on Jesus, then we have no need to worry or be troubled.

A Few Pitfalls

1. **Believing You Can Earn Your Way to Heaven by Being a Good Person.**

   Whether a person believes herself to be good or bad (based on comparison to others) is of no consequence. The issue is, is she willing to trust that Jesus is the only way to heaven. Or said another way, one does not have to be a good person to go to heaven. A person needs to acknowledge Jesus as Lord, confess her sins to Him, ask for forgiveness, and place her trust in Christ. Goodness or badness is not the issue. Further, good works is not the issue either. Good works will not gain us entrance to heaven.

2. **Thinking You Have to Trust Christ Again Each Time You Sin.**

   Trusting Christ is a one-time life-changing, eternity-altering decision. When we sin we need to confess it to the Lord in prayer to restore our fellowship with Him. However, our relationship with Him is secure because He does not leave when we sin.

3. **Doubting Your Sincerity When You Placed Your Faith in Christ.**

   This doubt troubles many sincere believers in Christ. I remember one woman I was discipling during a three-month mission trip to the Middle East. She shared with me that she constantly worried about her salvation and if she truly was saved. We talked about this in length. It became apparent to me this was a habit she had established that was deeply rooted. Like any habit we want to break, she needed to deny herself the temptation to think of her doubt each time it arose in her mind.

Like trying to stop chain smoking, the habit had to be denied.

She needed to replace the thoughts with either verses of Scripture, thoughts of goals in her life, or perhaps prayer for another person.

Over time, the habit will break and one can move on in security in one's relationship with God.

How to Begin a Relationship With God

This sample prayer was taken from the *Steps to Know God Personally* booklet by Cru (Campus Crusade for Christ).

Have you trusted that Jesus is the way to God?

o   If not would you like to do that today? If you never have done this, or you are a bit fuzzy on it, search your heart. See if this prayer expresses the desire of your heart and trust Christ's death on your behalf. If so, when did you trust Christ? Some people may not know a date, but they know they did this as a young child. Others, like me, can name the exact date of this decision because it happened at an older age. The bottom line is that this is not a decision to be taken lightly. I was fortunate to attend a reunion hosted at the church where I first put my faith in Christ. While there, I had my husband snap a picture of the pew where I knelt one Sunday evening and asked Jesus to forgive me of my sins, grant me eternal life with Him, and come into my life to make me the person He meant for me to be.

It hangs on my refrigerator, and I use it to teach my children that they, too, will make the same decision one day themselves.

Chapter 3: Jesus Promises the Holy Spirit

Digging Deeper

1. In John 14:16, 17, what term does Jesus use to refer to the Holy Spirit? (Helper, Spirit of truth). Your Bible might also say Counselor, Advocate, Comforter, etc.

2. According to John 14:17, where will the Holy Spirit reside? (In you.)

3. In John 16:7, who sends the Holy Spirit to us? (Jesus.)

4. In John 16:8, what will the Holy Spirit will do when He comes? (Convict the world concerning sin, righteousness and judgment.)

5. In John 16:13, what else will the Holy Spirit do? (Guide us into all truth, speak what He hears, disclose things of God to us.)

Just to be Clear

1. What pronoun is used to refer to the Holy Spirit? (He.)

For Further Study

1. In verses 4 and 5, what instructions did Jesus give the disciples? (Do not leave Jerusalem, wait for the promised gift from God (Father), the Holy Spirit.)

2. In verse 8, what two things did Jesus say would happen when the Holy Spirit came to the disciples? (Receive power and be My witnesses.)

3. What does it mean to be Jesus' witnesses? (To tell what you know about Jesus.) A witness simply tells what he heard or saw or knows concerning a situation. The disciples were Jesus' witnesses, to all who would listen, of all He had done on earth. We are now Jesus' witnesses when we share what we know of Jesus from the Bible and from His work in our lives.

4. In verses 2-4, what evidence do you see that something extraordinary was taking place? (A violent wind filled the house they were in, what looked like fire on top of their heads, they began to speak other languages.) This is one of my favorite stories in the book of Acts. The international crowd that was gathered for the Pentecost festival was able to hear the truth of God being proclaimed in their native tongues! What a powerful miraculous witness for Christ.

The Ongoing Role of the Holy Spirit

1. What are the things the "old you" wants to do (verses 19-21)? (Sexual immorality, impurity, debauchery, idolatry, witchcraft, hatred, discord, jealousy, fits of rage, selfish ambition, dissensions, factions, envy, drunkenness, orgies.)

Yep, that about covers all the areas my flesh (the old me) wants to get into.

2. What are the things the Holy Spirit wants to produce in your life (verse 22)? (Love, joy, peace, patience, kindness, goodness, faithfulness, gentleness, self-control.)

A Few Pitfalls

1. Not Allowing the Holy Spirit to Guide Your Life

Not letting the Holy Spirit have complete control in our lives is like having a million dollars in the bank and not utilizing it. Why would a person have riches in the bank and not use them somehow? In the same way, why would we have the God of the universe in our lives and not follow His lead? When we place our trust in Christ, we have God Himself, the Holy Spirit, now residing in our lives. God can see our future and lead us along the path He has destined for us. He will not force His gentle leading upon us; we must yield our will to His daily, even moment by moment.

2. Not Choosing the Fruit of the Spirit

I discipled a woman once who was not joyful in life. It seemed she lived with a frown and each day could focus only on what had gone wrong. Life was a chore for her to bear. One day I asked her why she was not joyful. I knew she had a personal relationship with Christ.

Since the Holy Spirit resided in her life, I was curious as to why she continued to live with such a sour attitude. I mentioned she had the choice—to choose to let the Holy Spirit produce the fruit of joy in her life. She said she never had thought of it that way. Weeks later we spoke again, and she told me she was choosing joy throughout the day instead of defaulting to her old habit of choosing to see life as a big downer. To see her approach life with a smile was amazing and quite a transformation!

Chapter 4: Jesus Teaches About Prayer

Digging Deeper

1. "Father" was a common way Jesus referred to His relationship with God while He was on earth. He prompted His disciples to refer to Him that way as well.

   o How does it make you feel that God wants you to address Him as Father? Knowing Jesus instructs His disciples to refer to God as Father really shows the type of intimate relationship God wants to have with us. He does not want or need servants/subjects/workers, but sons and daughters. The God of the universe wants me (and you) to call Him "Father."

2. This prayer begins with acknowledging who God is, acknowledging that He has a kingdom, and acknowledging we desire for His will to be done.

   o Why do you think it is key to begin our prayers with this in mind? God is God.

He is on His throne, He will reign forever, and He has a will and purpose for our lives. Taking that into account first, helps us keep our lives and events in perspective with God's ultimate and overall will.

   o How difficult or easy is it for you to ask for God's will to be done in your life? For me it depends on the area! Really I want God's will for me in each area, but it seems like some areas are easier to trust Him with than others.

3. According to this prayer, what are some things we can ask of God? We can ask for God's will to be done in our lives, daily bread (the things we need daily such as food, shelter, jobs), forgiveness of sins (the things we do wrong in our actions or thoughts or words or the things we neglect to do that God prompts us to do), the ability to forgive others that have wronged us, not to be lead into temptation, protection from the evil one (Satan), etc.

4. Forgiveness of sins is a key part of this prayer. Why do you think it is important to ask God to forgive our sins? We need to ask God to forgive our sins so that we keep open communication with Him. When we sin, we break our fellowship with God. He will not leave us, but to have the relationship repaired we need to acknowledge our sin, ask forgiveness, and repent (turn away from it).

Why should we also forgive others when they sin against us? It is hypocritical to ask God to forgive our sins when we refuse to forgive others for their sins against us. Another key reason we need to forgive others is that if we do not, we are the ones, in the end, who are hurt and eaten up with hate and bitterness.

Just to be Clear

1. Does this passage mention a certain time of day you need to pray? (No.)

2. Does this passage mention you need to be in a certain place when you pray? (No.)

3. Does this passage mention a certain position you need to be in to pray? (No.)

For Further Study

1. In verses 1-5, Jesus is praying for Himself.

o In verse 4, how did Jesus bring glory to God? (By completing the work God gave Him to do.)

o In verse 5, what time period does Jesus refer to? (The time before the world began.)

2. In verse 6-18, Jesus prays for His disciples.

o Who does Jesus say He is protecting us from (verse 15)? (The evil one.) Another great passage on the subject of protection is Psalm 91. I regularly pray portions of this passage for myself and my family.

3. In verses 20-26, Jesus prays for future believers.

o In verse 20, who is Jesus praying for? (Those who would believe in Him.)

A Few Pitfalls

1. Using Eloquent Language or Strange Words in Prayer

Using fancy words or words that sound religious are not needed in prayer.

Just talking to God in your normal tone with words you normally would use is best.

2. Using Repetitive Words in Prayer

God hears your prayers the first time you utter them, (He even knows your heart before you speak), so repeating words or phrases is not necessary.

3. Saying the Same Scripted Prayer Repeatedly Each Day

Anytime you pray, you want to mean it. Words on a paper are nothing. It is the meaning you put into your prayers that makes them personal.

4. Thinking God Does Not Want to be Bothered by Your Prayers

Whether it is about a parking spot, an upcoming test, a flight, even needed healing for a friend or loved one, you can pray for anything and everything.

5. Not Realizing How Unforgiveness Is a Pitfall to Prayer

It seems that hurt and anger come to the surface and distracts us when we want to talk to God. It is best to deal with the hurt and unforgiveness so there are no distractions in our prayers.

Chapter 5: Jesus Uses Scripture

Digging Deeper

1. What did Jesus say as a response to Satan each time Satan tempted him? (Scripture from the Old Testament, God's Word.)

2. Why do you think Satan tempted Jesus to turn stones into bread? (Jesus had been fasting, so was likely very hungry.)

3. Satan used Scripture to tempt Jesus.

o According to this passage, does Satan know Scripture? (Yes, he does.) He twists Scripture to try and confuse us and tempt us to sin.

o What is the difference between how Satan used Scripture and how Jesus used Scripture? (Satan used God's Word to tempt Jesus to stumble. Jesus used Scripture to obey God and to keep from sinning.)

4. When Satan showed Jesus all the kingdoms of the world, what did Satan want Jesus to do? (Bow down and worship him.)

For Further Study

1. What does this verse say Scripture is useful for?

(Teaching, rebuking, correcting, and training in righteous-ness for equipping for good works.)

2. How do you think the Bible corrects us (verse 16)? (It teaches right and wrong in many areas of life.) When we compare our lives to the Bible, we can see areas that need adjusting to line up more with God's Word. When we come to a passage of Scripture, such as James 2:1, "My brothers, as believers in our glorious Lord Jesus Christ, don't show favoritism," we can stop and think, "Do I show favoritism? Do I treat people equally with respect, or do I treat some people with less respect?" For example, do I treat my check-er at Walmart like a doormat, but treat my pastor like a king? We need to treat people like God does, with love and respect, regardless of their earthly job or status or riches. So that is one of many ways the Bible is so very helpful in teaching us and correcting us.

3. How does the Bible equip us for every good work? (The Bible teaches us the very things God wants us to focus on in life.) Loving Him, loving our neighbor as our self, for-giving others, giving, taking care of widows and orphans (James 1:27), are just a few.

How the Bible (Canon) Came Together

As for the Old Testament, Hebrew believers recognized God's messengers and accepted their writings as inspired of God. While there undeniably was some debate in regard to the Old Testament canon, by A.D. 250 there was nearly universal agreement on the canon of Hebrew Scripture.

For the New Testament, the process of the recognition and collec-tion began in the first centuries of the Christian church.

Very early on, some of the New Testament books were being recognized. Paul considered Luke's writings to be as authoritative as the Old Testament (1 Timothy 5:18; see also Deuteronomy 25:4 and Luke 10:7). Peter recognized Paul's writings as Scripture (2 Peter 3:15-16). Some of the books of the New Testament were being circulated among the churches (Colossians 4:16; 1 Thessalonians 5:27). Clement of Rome mentioned at least eight New Testament books (A.D. 95). Ignatius of Antioch acknowledged approximately seven books (A.D. 115). Polycarp, a disciple of John the apostle*, acknowledged 15 books (A.D. 108). Later, Irenaeus mentioned 21 books (A.D. 185). Hippolytus recognized 22 books (A.D. 170-235).

The Council of Hippo (A.D. 393) and the Council of Carthage (A.D. 397) affirmed 27 books as authoritative.

These councils followed something similar to the following principles to determine whether a New Testament book truly was inspired by the Holy Spirit:

1. Was the author an apostle or have a close connection with an apostle?

2. Was the book being accepted by the body of Christ at large?

3. Did the book contain consistency of doctrine and orthodox teaching?

4. Did the book bear evidence of high moral and spiritual values that would reflect a work of the Holy Spirit?

Again, it is crucial to remember that the church did not determine the canon. No early church council decided on the canon. It was God, and God alone, who determined which books belonged in the Bible. It was simply a matter of God imparting to His followers what He already had decided.

Taken from the article "How and When was the Canon of the Bible Put Together?" by CEO, S. Michael Houdmann at www.GotQuestions.org

A Few Pitfalls

1. **Since the Bible has been translated so many times, how do I know that the version I have is trustworthy?**

   I hear this most often. No need to let this trip you up. If you ever read a King James Bible, you will be glad that newer Bibles have been translated (using dependable manuscripts written in the original language) into how we speak today.

2. **The Bible is such a big book, I don't know where to start, I am overwhelmed by it.**

   Bible commentaries can be a great help. I use an online commentary called SonicLight (http://www.soniclight.com/). I also have a two-volume set I keep handy called *The Bible Knowledge Commentary* by Walvoord and Zuck.

   I also have a *Life Application Bible* that has a Bible commentary built into the Bible. So when I come across a passage of Scripture that is confusing to me, I simply pull out one of these resources and look up what Bible scholars say it means. These resources can be purchased online and in Christian bookstores. Take your time to choose one you can understand.

3. **I am too busy to read the Bible.**

A great way to read the Bible in just a few minutes a day is to use a one-year Bible version. It breaks the Bible down into daily readings of bite-sized chunks. Consider reading it with a highlighter and marking things that stand out to you each day.

START HERE

Chapter 6: Jesus Gives the Great Commission

Digging Deeper

1. What did Jesus tell His disciples to do in verses 19 and 20? (Go and make disciples of all the nations, baptizing them, teaching them to obey all the commands He had given.)

2. What does Jesus assure them of in verse 20? (To be with them.)

For Further Study

1. Compare these verses (Mark 16:15, 16) with the verses from Matthew 28:18-20. List any similarities. (Both use the word "go," and both talk about baptism.) We are also supposed to get out there, tell others about Christ, and be His witnesses in our spheres of influence and to other nations.

2. Compare the verses again and list any differences. (Matthew says to make disciples of all nations. Mark says to preach the good news to all creation. Mark says those who do not believe the good news will be condemned.)

Just to be Clear

1. In the first passage, is making disciples a mere suggestion? (No.)

2. Is there any reference in this passage about having to be a pastor, a vocational missionary, or needing a theology degree before telling others about Christ? (No.) Anyone who puts his or her faith in Christ is His witness and can share about Him to others. A vocational missionary is a person whose entire job (what they are paid for) is to share the love of God and salvation in Christ with others, whether here in the U.S. or internationally. However, we all are missionaries in the sense that we can share with others about our faith in Christ wherever we go: work, school, coffee shops, neighborhoods, etc.

3. Is there any reference to keeping silent and hoping someone will ask us about our faith in Jesus? (No.) Both passages are clear about our responsibility to go and share with those who have not heard about Jesus Christ, His life, death, and resurrection, and the eternal life He offers through a relationship with Him.

A Few Pitfalls

1. **Erroneously believing you have to know a lot to tell others about Christ**

   We never will be an expert on the things of God. So do not ever let that hold you back from telling others about Christ.

2. **Leaving the Great Commission work to professional career missionaries**

This can be a way Satan may try to keep you from sharing the good news with others. He might tempt you to play it safe and not share about Jesus saying, "Oh, leave that to people who do that as their full-time job."

3. **Wondering if your salvation story is dramatic enough to share with others**

Again, this can merely be a ploy from Satan to try and keep you silent about what Jesus has done in your life. Your story is special because it is a personal account of God doing a wonderful work in your life! Celebrate that and share it with others.

START HERE

A Special Note to the Small Group Leader and Discipler

I am so proud of you for taking a step of faith to love on and disciple another woman in her growing relationship with Christ. Whether in a small group or one-to-one, I know you will enjoy being God's instrument in another's life.

I have written these Bible study lessons based on my many years of helping new believers grow in Christ. I have seen and used tons of different Bible studies in an effort to help women get started on the right foot in their new life in Christ. I stand on the work of others who have gone before me in the same endeavor and have fashioned this series after what I wish I would have had on the field years ago and what I want to have as a tool in my hands now.

As you get started in this study I encourage you to do the lesson yourself first, on your own. Look up the verses, answer the questions, and see what personal stories the Lord may bring to your mind for you to share with the woman/women you meet with. If you are meeting with a woman one-to-one, you then can sit down with her and work through the lesson together (or she could have done it herself before you meet together) and discuss your answers. If you get stumped, please refer to some of my thoughts in the back of the book. If you want further help in discipleship please contact me on my Facebook page www.facebook.com/disciplingwomen or my website www.disciplingwomen.com.

You may also find it helpful to get a copy of my book *Discipling Women* to help you in all areas of discipleship.

Again, great job! Way to go! Stepping out in faith and asking the Lord to use you in the life of another is a wonderful, thrilling journey!

By His Grace,

Lori

START HERE

A Special Note to First Time Readers

Hi there! When I first put my faith in Christ years ago, I was fortunate enough to have a loving couple step into my life and help me find my way. My youth director at the church I was attending lovingly shared the message of God's love and forgiveness, and I put my faith in Christ. He and his wife then began to nurture me, teach me, and model for me what it meant to walk with God and fall more in love with Christ each day.

I am thrilled that you want to grow in your relationship with Christ. Each of the Bible studies is designed to help you be nurtured, loved on, taught how to walk with God, and grow in your relationship with Christ. You might be new in your relationship with Christ or never really received help after you put your faith in Christ, or perhaps you have gotten off track somewhere. My prayer is that this book will help.

These are foundational lessons that will help as you begin walking with Christ. They will explore basic beliefs in the Christian faith such as *God's love, Jesus is the way to God, prayer, the Holy Spirit,* and others. As you learn and grow, God eventually will use you to help another grow in Christ, so take good notes. This book will become your very own leader's guide for the woman you disciple one day!

If you have any questions, ask your discipler.* If you do not have someone discipling you, ask your church or ministry leadership to recommend someone to come alongside you.

You are, of course, welcome to contact me on my Facebook page www.facebook.com/disciplingwomen or my website www.disciplingwomen.com.

Blessings On Your Journey,

Lori

START HERE

Spending Time With God

Spending personal time with God on a regular basis will be paramount for your continued growth in your relationship with Him. He loves you, created you, has plans for you, and desires a relationship with you. Can you even believe it! The God of the universe is personal?! It is amazing and hard to even comprehend.

The items below are not exhaustive. They are just a loose framework—a jumping off point—to help you get started. There is no formula here. These are simply some ideas to help you connect with God.

Why Spend Time With God

There are numerous reasons to put a regular appointment with God in your daily schedule. This is a time where you can get to know Him. Just like in a love relationship with a significant other, or a best friend, we get to know people by spending time with them. It is the same with God, the more time spent with Him, the more we really know Him. Also, this time together with God provides a regular place for you to ask for His guidance in areas of your life, to ask for His wisdom to help you navigate tough decisions and to lay your requests, needs and wants before Him.

Where to Spend Time With God

This can be just about anywhere you can imagine where you are able to concentrate on being with God. Options include places like at your dining room table, on the couch, in your bedroom, or even at your desk. You could also choose a nearby park, your porch, a rocking chair by a warm fire, or your favorite chair. I even have spent time with God in coffee shops and on flights.

When to Spend Time With God

Some people have a very regular time with God, like say 6:00-7:00 a.m. each morning. They have built that into their schedules, and that is the best time to meet with God for them. Others adjust the time with Him and the length of time based on stage of life.

I have done all of the above! In college I spent time every night before bed with God. I greatly enjoyed, at the end of a day, reading my Bible and praying to Him and giving Him my worries and fears and hopes for the future. This time with Him was very comforting to me and brought me great peace during the hectic pace of college pressures. I would read a chapter of the Bible each night and by the end of college, had made my way through the Bible completely. God spoke to me through His Word, and that regular time with Him shaped my life.

After college that time moved to early morning. I found a routine that worked very well for me during my single, working years. I would wake up early and go straight to the gym and work out. Then I would come home, shower, and eat breakfast with Jesus.

I would make breakfast and then spend time with God in the quietness of my apartment. I did this for years—like a regular breakfast date!

As a mom of little ones, it became tough to find a new routine that worked. Each stage of my children's life, from newborn to kindergarten, has been a challenge to find a quiet time with just me and God. Currently, I wake up before the boys do (or let them quietly watch cartoons) while I spend time with God in devotion and prayer.

Depending on where you are at in life, any one of these scenarios might work for you:

o   For a college student: in between classes or early before classes begin or at the end of the day, in your bed before going to sleep.

o   For a young mom: during the children's naps.

o For a working woman: at your desk before the work day begins.

o Imagine a circle around you and spend time with God on long flights, in coffee shops, or with a roommate nearby.

What to do When Spending Time With God

Some basic general elements that can be included in your time with God include Bible reading, prayer, worship, study, and perhaps journaling. Time with Him is not a formula nor a list of do's and don'ts; it is building a relationship, so don't get too legalistic here.

Bible Reading

Reading the Bible is a foundational part of any time spent with God because His Word, the Scriptures, is His primary way of revealing Himself to us. We learn more about God, His character, His love for us, and His hatred of sin by reading the Bible.

We learn about heaven, hell, Jesus, etc.

o Consider purchasing the **One Year Bible.** This is a fantastic way to read through the Bible in one year. Each day's reading is about 15 minutes.

o Purchase a study Bible. This Bible has notes written on each page explaining each verse, what it means, and how to apply to daily life. I own the **Life Application Bible**.

o Read a chapter of the Bible each day, starting in the Gospels—perhaps the Gospel of John.

o Subscribe to online Bible reading plans. Some sites email you Bible readings each day. Two that I have used are: www.odb.org and www.biblegateway.com/reading-plans

o Search and download one of the many Bible reading apps available for phones and tablets.

Prayer

The primary way we communicate with God is through prayer. Prayer is simply talking to God. Talking with Him out loud or in our hearts/minds is such an important part of our fellowship with Him.

- o Consider using the Lord's Prayer as a model. In Luke 11:1-4, we read how Jesus taught His disciples how to pray. Consider reading each line and talking to God about that subject. For example, "Lead us not into temptation" (v.4) would be a place you could ask God to help you with a particular temptation you are dealing with.

- o ACTS: This is a simple guide to help you organize your prayers. "A"—adoration, where we praise God for who He is. "C"—confession, where we confess any known sin to Him and ask for forgiveness. "T"—thanksgiving, where we thank Him for the many blessings in our lives. "S"—supplication (short for supply), where we ask God to supply for us the things we need (large or small).

- o Prayer list: This is a simple list of things or people you are praying for. I have a small index card that lists on Mondays I specifically pray for each family member, on Tuesdays I pray for people who I hope with put their faith in Christ, on Wednesdays I pray for co-workers, etc.

- o Journaling: Many people like to write out their prayers in a journal. I personally love to write in journals and have tons of journals filled with letters to God.

I greatly enjoy looking back at these journals to read where God answered a specific prayer, how He changed my heart in an area, etc.

Worship

There are many, many ways to worship the Lord. Singing praise songs to God or listening to worship music are just a few.

I currently have a particular song I like to use to start my time with Him.

- o Download worship music to listen to during your time alone with Him.

- o If you do not currently own any worship music, head to the nearest Christian bookstore and ask for some recommendations.

- o As you sing, think about the words and meditate on Jesus and your love for Him and His love for you.

Study

Is there a topic you would like to know more about such as prayer, heaven/hell, angels, miracles or parables of Christ? Or perhaps you want to learn more about a particular book of the Bible. You can use this time to dive deeper into those topics/books.

- o Go to a Christian bookstore and peruse the Bible study materials for topics or books that interest you.

- o Search a topic online and purchase via the Internet. Sometimes you will be a part of a Bible study on a particular topic, and that Bible study will have "homework" for you to do during your time with God.

Time alone with God each day will help you deepen your relationship with Him. Making this a part of your daily routine will yield a closer walk with Christ over time.

For me, after I spend time with God, I then keep in regular contact with Him throughout the day. In my heart, wherever I am, I am talking with Him, confessing sin, praying for a friend, and whispering my love for Him.

START HERE

Leading a Small Group Bible Study

Leading a small group Bible study can be such a thrill! Allowing God to use you to facilitate a learning environment for a group of women is a fantastic way to see them grow in their relationship with God. Here are a few simple elements of a small group Bible study that will help yours be a success.

Welcome/Icebreaker

This helps the Bible study time start by opening with a fun question to get the women talking and interacting. For example, you may want to say something such as, "Welcome ladies! I am thrilled you all are here! To start us off, I thought we could go around the room (table, etc.) and share a highlight from last week." If you want to tie the question into the lesson, you could say, "This week our lesson was about how Jesus demonstrates God's love. When you think of a person in your life who really loves you, who would that be?" If a holiday is approaching, you could say, "What is a tradition your family practices during the Thanksgiving season?" The great thing about an easy ice breaker question is that there is no right or wrong answer. Women new in their faith or new to the Bible study can answer freely without feeling any pressure to know something about the Bible.

Announcements

I like to do any type of business things, announcements, etc., toward the beginning of the small group time so the second half of the time can be focused on the Lord and prayer and what He is doing in women's lives. For example, I may say, "Hey ladies, don't forget that next week we will not have Bible study since it is Spring Break. We will pick up the next week with Chapter 3."

I might add, "Don't forget to bring perishable food items, baby formula, and diapers for the women's shelter donation we are preparing."

Vision of Bible Study

This answers the question: Why are we meeting? This varies group to group. Some groups are part of a church or other ministry; some are led by women of all ages simply wanting to help others around them grow in the Lord. I have led groups from my home, in dorms, in gyms where I worked out, and in other people's homes.

The vision of the group needs simply to state what the group is about and what you are trying to accomplish. Here are some I have used over the years.

o "The vision of this group is to help women grow in Christ. It is my vision that each of you will grow in Christ and gain valuable tools to use in your walk with Him. Also, it is my vision that you each will, one day, lead your own group. Through that you and I can make a real impact for Christ in our city."

o "The vision of the group is to grow and multiply to reach out to more people. As new folks come into this fellowship and put their faith in Christ and grow in Him, I pray that we will outgrow this place. I pray we will need to multiply into smaller groups, meeting at more than one location, to be able to continually involve and make room for new people."

o "My heart is to see each of you developed as women leaders in your church, leading other women to Christ and discipling them in the Lord. This Bible study serves as a catalyst and step to that end.

Content/Discussion

At this point lead the group to talk about and discuss the lesson. There are two ways to do this. One way is when the ladies come to the group with the lesson completed. They have looked up the biblical passages and answered the questions at home, on their own. They come to group ready to talk about that chapter. In this case you, as the Bible study leader, could ask questions such as, "What stood out to you this week?" "What passages did you have questions about or wanted further explanation for?" "On page 15, it talked about pitfalls in this area. Does anyone have a story to share about that, perhaps one of the pitfalls you have experienced in the past?"

You could share a story reflecting how this lesson has affected you personally or a story from your life that goes along with the topic.

Another way to do the Content/Discussion part of the small group Bible study is to complete the lesson together as a group. Take turns reading the passages, looking up the verses, and answering the questions. You might say, "Lindsey, would you mind reading the passage background and verse out loud?" After she reads it anyone can answer the questions and discuss thoughts. Then say, "Becky, can you read the pitfalls?" After she reads, ask, "Has anyone ever fallen into one of those? Are any of these surprising to you?"

o   If someone continually answers all the questions, simply say, "On this next question, I would love to hear from a few of you who have not had a chance to share yet."

o   If someone answers a question incorrectly, you can say, "Let's look again at the passage. What does it say?" or "Does anyone else have any thoughts on that?" or "I can see where you are coming from, but in this passage (or lesson) the answer is …"

Prayer

This is an important step in a small group Bible study for many reasons. The study is a place where we can communicate with God and ask Him to help us apply the things we learned in the study. It also is a place where we can show care for each other by praying to God about each other's needs. Further, it is a great place to model prayer, especially for newer believers when they hear you pray in real, authentic ways. Here are some of the ways I have approached prayer in Bible studies over the years.

- o Have each person share a prayer requests or two. Then have each person pray for someone else in the group. You could say, "How about if each person prays for the person on your right, and I will close our prayer time."

- o Divide folks up into groups of two and have them share requests and pray for each other.

- o Just pray. Say, "I am going to start us, and as we go around the circle in prayer, please pray for whatever is on your heart today." In this example you do not share the requests first. Women just pray out loud to God and can include requests of Him if needed.

A section to record specific prayer requests is at the end of each chapter in **Start Here**. You may want to give time, periodically, for women to go back and review past prayer requests and see which ones God has answered so far.

Snacks

I always provide some type of snack or drink in my small groups. There is something about food that brings women together, creates a familiar environment, and gets them talking.

You can either provide this yourself or let women sign up to bring snacks on a particular week. When you sit down to plan your Bible study, simply refer to that sheet to see who is bringing snacks. You may need to send an email reminder.

Planning for your Small Group Bible Study

Having a plan and being prepared will give you confidence as you lead your small group and help you make it successful. I like to prepare for each Bible study a few days before it happens so I can make sure I am ready and have everything I need. I have included a planning worksheet from my own files for you to use. Before I start, though, I slip down on my knees and pray. I ask God to direct my thoughts as I plan. I fully realize I cannot change lives. I only can facilitate an environment where God is worshipped, adored, and where He can work in the lives of the women who will be in attendance. I ask the Holy Spirit to fill me to over flowing. I pray will have the mind of Christ as I prepare. I seek to stay in step for what He has for the group that week. Then, confident of God's leading, I pull out my Bible study planning worksheet and prepare.

There are blanks beside each element of the small group. That is because over time I begin to delegate out different tasks of the small group. I like to give others opportunity to lead in small ways (do the vision or icebreaker questions) in hopes they will grow in their ability to lead and one day lead their own group!

I will contact a particular woman and say, "Hi Charlotte! I am planning for Bible study on Wednesday and wondered if you will lead the prayer portion of our time together?" She may need some help or direction. During the Bible study I say, "I asked Charlotte to lead our prayer time today."

As you see an up–and-coming leader in the group, you may consider having her sit with you as you plan your small group. Let her see the planning page, how you decide each element, and who will do what. Let her see how you plan, what questions you will ask in discussion, what prayer idea you will implement that week, etc.

Your group will be a success if you let God lead in your heart and mind the best you can and prepare for your group instead of "winging" it last minute. It is my hope that your small group helps women's lives change for Him, and in turn they make a difference for Christ in their communities.

Bible Study Planning Worksheet

Date: _____

Welcome/Icebreaker: _____

Announcements: _____

Vision of Bible Study : _____

Content/Discussion: _____

Prayer: _____

Snacks: _____